Presented To:

_____

Presented By:

_____

Date:

_____

GOD'S LITTLE INSTRUCTION BOOK FOR MOM

Honor Books
Tulsa, Oklahoma

God's Little Instruction Book for Mom
ISBN 1-56292-860-0
Copyright © 2000 by Honor Books
P. O. Box 55388
Tulsa, Oklahoma 74155

Introduction

God's Little Instruction Book for Mom is an inspirational collection of quotes and scriptures that will motivate you to live a meaningful, productive, and happy life—while meeting and enjoying the challenges of being a mom.

Some books have quotes and some have scriptures, but we have combined both to provide not just human wisdom but also God's insights into one of life's most challenging jobs: being a mom. This little book will give you much to ponder and much to enjoy—especially the last section, which offers a collection of humorous and witty quotations that you'll want to share with other moms.

God's Little Instruction Book for Mom covers topics that mothers around the world can relate to, and it's a welcome break from the fast-paced frenzy of everyday life. We hope that you enjoy and treasure this book as much as we do.

*M*others are like fine collectibles—as the years go by they increase in value.

Despise not thy mother when she is old.

PROVERBS 23:22

*T*rain your child in the way
in which you know you should
have gone yourself.

I will instruct thee and teach thee in the way which thou shalt go:
I will guide thee with mine eye.

PSALM 32:8

*A*s a mother, my job is to take care of the possible and trust God with the impossible.

And they that know thy name will put their trust in thee: for thou, LORD, hast not forsaken them that seek thee.

PSALM 9:10

*W*hen Mother Theresa received her Nobel Prize, she was asked, "What can we do to promote world peace?" She replied, "Go home and love your family."

Let love and faithfulness never leave you; bind them around
your neck, write them on the tablet of your heart.

PROVERBS 3:3 NIV

You built no great cathedrals
That centuries applaud,
But with a grace exquisite
Your life cathedraled God.

Ye are the temple of the living God; as God hath said,
I will dwell in them, and walk in them.

2 CORINTHIANS 6:16

*W*here parents do too much for their children, the children will not do much for themselves.

The soul of the sluggard desireth, and hath nothing: but the soul of the diligent shall be made fat.

PROVERBS 13:4

If we as parents are too busy
to listen to our children,
how then can they understand
a God who hears?

Let the wise listen.

PROVERBS 1:5 NIV

*N*ever, never be too proud to say, "I'm sorry" to your child when you've made a mistake.

Confess your faults one to another, and pray one for another.

JAMES 5:16

*T*here's a time when you have to explain to your children why they're born, and it's a marvelous thing if you know the reason.

Before I (God) formed thee in the belly I knew thee; and before thou camest forth out of the womb I sanctified thee, and I ordained thee.

JEREMIAH 1:5

If a child lives with approval,
he learns to live with himself.

Accept one another, just as Christ also
accepted us to the glory of God.

ROMANS 15:7 NASB

The highest pinnacle of the spiritual life is not joy in unbroken sunshine but absolute and undoubting trust in the love of God.

Whatsoever is born of God overcometh the world: and this is the victory that overcometh the world, even our faith.

1 JOHN 5:4

A mother has, perhaps, the hardest earthly lot; and yet no mother worthy of the name ever gave herself thoroughly for her child who did not feel that, after all, she reaped what she had sown.

Let us not be weary in well doing: for in due season we shall reap, if we faint not.

GALATIANS 6:9

Simply having children does not make mothers.

Teach the young women to be sober . . . to love their children.

TITUS 2:4

A mother once asked a clergyman when she should begin the education of her child, . . . "Madam," was the reply, . . . "From the very first smile that gleams over an infant's cheek, your opportunity begins."

Train up a child in the way he should go,
Even when he is old he will not depart from it.

PROVERBS 22:6 NASB

19

*L*oving a child is a circular
business . . . the more you give,
the more you get, the more
you get, the more you give.

Give, and it will be given to you. . . . For by your standard
of measure it will be measured to you in return.

LUKE 6:38 NASB

*I*f you want your child to accept your values when he reaches his teen years, then you must be worthy of his respect during his younger days.

In order to offer ourselves as a model for you,
that you might follow our example.

2 THESSALONIANS 3:9 NASB

*W*omen should not have children after thirty-five—thirty-five children are enough.

Happy is the man that hath his quiver full of them.

PSALM 127:5

When we set an example of honesty our children will be honest. When we encircle them with love they will be loving. When we practice tolerance they will be tolerant. When we meet life with laughter and a twinkle in our eye they will develop a sense of humor.

Be thou an example of the believers, in word, in conversation, in charity, in spirit, in faith, in purity.

1 TIMOTHY 4:12

A happy childhood is one of the best gifts that parents have it in their power to bestow.

Withhold not good from them to whom it is due,

when it is in the power of thine hand to do it.

PROVERBS 3:27

The family tree is worth bragging about if it has consistently produced good timber, and not just nuts.

A good name is rather to be chosen than great riches.

PROVERBS 22:1

*T*here is only one pretty child
in the world, and every
mother has it.

He hath made every thing beautiful in his time.

ECCLESIASTES 3:11

*T*he mother's love is like God's love;
He loves us not because we are loveable,
but because it is His nature to love,
and because we are His children.

Herein is love, not that we loved God, but that he loved us,
and sent his Son to be the propitiation for our sins. Beloved,
if God so loved us, we ought also to love one another.

1 JOHN 4:10,11

Children spell "love" T-I-M-E.

Don't be fools; be wise: make the most of every
opportunity you have for doing good.

EPHESIANS 5:16 TLB

In practicing the art of
parenthood an ounce of example
is worth a ton of preachment.

Let your light so shine before men, that they may see your
good works, and glorify your Father which is in heaven.

MATTHEW 5:16

*C*hildren are God's apostles,
day by day sent forth to preach
of love and hope and peace.

Behold, children are a gift of the LORD.

PSALM 127:3 NASB

If it is desirable that children be kind, appreciative, and pleasant, those qualities should be taught—not hoped for.

The commandment is a lamp; and the law is light;
and reproofs of instruction are the way of life.

PROVERBS 6:23

A child is fed with
milk and praise.

Let no corrupt communication proceed out of your mouth,
but that which is good to the use of edifying, that
it may minister grace unto the hearers.

EPHESIANS 4:29

A mother is neither cocky, nor proud, because she knows the school principal may call at any minute to report that her child has just driven a motorcycle through the gymnasium.

Boast not thyself of tomorrow; for thou knowest not what a day may bring forth.

PROVERBS 27:1

*H*ome is the place where
the great are small and
the small are great.

Many that are first shall be last; and the last shall be first.

MATTHEW 19:30

You are never so high as when you are on your knees.

Humble yourselves in the sight of the Lord, and he shall lift you up.

JAMES 4:10

*W*hen home is ruled according to God's Word, angels might be asked to stay with us, and they would not find themselves out of their element.

I will meditate in thy precepts, and have respect unto thy ways.
I will delight myself in thy statutes: I will not forget thy word.

PSALM 119:15-16

The best things you can give
children, next to good habits,
are good memories.

The memory of the just is blessed.

PROVERBS 10:7

*T*hrough the ages no nation
has had a better friend than
the mother who taught
her child to pray.

Devote yourselves to prayer, keeping alert in it with an attitude of thanksgiving.

COLOSSIANS 4:2 NASB

*G*ive your troubles to God;
He will be up all night anyway.

He will not allow your foot to slip; He who keeps you will not slumber.

PSALM 121:3 NASB

*W*e should seize every opportunity to give encouragement. Encouragement is oxygen to the soul.

A man hath joy by the answer of his mouth:
and a word spoken in due season, how good is it!

PROVERBS 15:23

You know children are growing up
when they start asking
questions that have answers.

When I was a child, I spake as a child, I understood as a child, I thought
as a child: but when I became a man, I put away childish things.

1 CORINTHIANS 13:11

*I*f you want a baby, have a new one.
Don't baby the old one.

Chasten thy son while there is hope, and
let not thy soul spare for his crying.

PROVERBS 19:18

*N*ever despair of a child. The one you weep the most for at the mercy-seat may fill your heart with the sweetest joys.

He that goeth forth and weepeth, bearing precious seed,

shall doubtless come again with rejoicing.

PSALM 126:6

*A*ll that I am or hope to be,
I owe to my mother.

Get all the advice you can and be wise the rest of your life.

PROVERBS 19:20 TLB

The best academy, a mother's knee.

Discipline your son, and he will give you peace;
he will bring delight to your soul.

PROVERBS 29:17 NIV

*M*other means selfless devotion,
limitless sacrifice, and
love that passes understanding.

Greater love hath no man than this,
that a man lay down his life for his friends.

JOHN 15:13

You may give without loving, but you cannot love without giving.

For God so loved the world, that he gave his only begotten Son, that whosoever believeth in him should not perish, but have everlasting life.

JOHN 3:16

A mother is a person who sees that there are only four pieces
of pie for five persons and promptly
remarks that she's never cared for pie.

It is more blessed to give than to receive.

ACTS 20:35

What is a home without a Bible?
'Tis a home where daily
bread for the body is provided,
but the soul is never fed.

My son, attend to my words; incline thine ear unto my sayings. Let them not depart from thine eyes; keep them in the midst of thine heart. For they are life unto those that find them, and health to all their flesh.

PROVERBS 4:20-22

A torn jacket is soon mended; but hard words bruise the heart of a child.

In accordance with the authority which the Lord gave me,
for building up and not for tearing down.

2 C O R I N T H I A N S   13:10   N A S B

A mother is not a person to lean on, but a person to make leaning unnecessary.

Therefore shall a man leave his father and his mother,
and shall cleave unto his wife: and they shall be one flesh.

GENESIS 2:24

*O*f all the rights of women,
the greatest is to be a mother.

Her children arise up, and call her blessed;
her husband also, and he praiseth her.

PROVERBS 31:28

*C*hildren miss nothing in sizing
up their parents. If you are
only half convinced of your beliefs,
they will quickly discern that fact.

Let us hold fast the profession of our faith without wavering.

HEBREWS 10:23

An infallible way to make
your child miserable is to
satisfy all his demands.

The rod and reproof give wisdom: but a child left
to himself bringeth his mother to shame.

PROVERBS 29:15

*D*ear Mother—You know that nothing
can ever change what we have always
been and will always be
to each other.

Her children stand and bless her.

PROVERBS 31:28 TLB

*B*abies are such a nice way
to start people.

She conceived . . . and said, I have gotten a man from the LORD.

GENESIS 4:1

*W*hen I come to the end of my rope,
God is there to take over.

He hath said, I will never leave thee, nor forsake thee.

HEBREWS 13:5

A mother understands what a child does not say.

Serve him with a perfect heart and with a willing mind:
for the LORD searcheth all hearts, and understandeth
all the imaginations of the thoughts.

1 CHRONICLES 28:9

*C*hildren are natural mimics—they act like their parents in spite of every attempt to teach them good manners.

Beloved, follow not that which is evil, but that which is good.

3 JOHN 11

*T*he Lord can do great things through those who don't care who gets the credit.

A man's pride shall bring him low: but honour
shall uphold the humble in spirit.

PROVERBS 29:23

A little boy's mother once told
him that it is God who makes
people good. He looked up and replied,
"Yes I know it is God,
but mothers help a lot."

Reject not nor forsake the teaching of your mother.

PROVERBS 1:8 AMP

*W*hat sunshine is to flowers, smiles
are to humanity. They are but trifles,
to be sure but, scattered along
life's pathway, the good they
do is inconceivable.

A happy heart makes the face cheerful.

PROVERBS 15:13 NIV

I regret often that I have spoken; never that I have been silent.

In the multitude of words there wanteth not sin:
but he that refraineth his lips is wise.

PROVERBS 10:19

Children are likely to live up to
what you believe of them.

As he thinketh in his heart, so is he.

PROVERBS 23:7

Children are the hands by which we take hold of heaven.

Verily I say unto you, Whosoever shall not receive the kingdom of God as a little child shall in no wise enter therein.

LUKE 18:17

*T*he persons hardest to convince they're at the retirement age are children at bedtime.

Correct thy son, and he shall give thee rest; yea,

he shall give delight unto thy soul.

PROVERBS 29:17

*M*any parents are finding out
that a pat on the back helps develop
character—if given often enough,
early enough, and low enough.

*He that spareth his rod hateth his son: but he
that loveth him chasteneth him betimes.*

PROVERBS 13:24

"*I* can forgive, but I cannot forget,"
is only another way of saying,
"I will not forgive." Forgiveness ought
to be like a canceled note—torn
in two, and burned up, so that it
never can be shown against one.

Be ye kind one to another, tenderhearted, forgiving one another,
even as God for Christ's sake hath forgiven you.

EPHESIANS 4:32

*B*eing a full time mother is one
of the highest salaried jobs
in my field since the
payment is pure love.

Whatsoever a man soweth, that shall he also reap.

GALATIANS 6:7

*M*otherhood is a partnership with God.

For this child I prayed; and the LORD hath given me my petition which
I asked of him: Therefore also I have lent him to the LORD;
as long as he liveth he shall be lent to the Lord.

1 SAMUEL 1:27-28

Children need love, especially when they do not deserve it.

Be ye therefore merciful, as your Father also is merciful.

LUKE 6:36

*T*oo much love never spoils children. Children become spoiled when we substitute "presents" for "presence."

We loved you so much that we were delighted to share with you
not only the gospel of God but our lives as well,
because you had become so dear to us.

1 THESSALONIANS 2:8 NIV

A man's work is from
sun to sun, but a mother's
work is never done.

Her candle goeth not out by night.

PROVERBS 31:18

*W*orry is like a rocking chair:
It gives you something to do,
but doesn't get you anywhere.

Casting the whole of your care [all your anxieties, all your worries,
all your concerns, once and for all] on Him, for He cares
for you affectionately and cares about you watchfully.

1 PETER 5:7 AMP

*I*f you have no prayer life
yourself, it is rather a useless
gesture to make your child
say his prayers every night.

Pray without ceasing.

1 THESSALONIANS 5:17

*T*he darn trouble with cleaning the house is it gets dirty the next day anyway, so skip a week if you have to. The children are the most important thing.

Lo, children are an heritage of the LORD:
and the fruit of the womb is his reward.

PSALM 127:3

If there is anything we wish to change in the child, we should first examine it and see whether it is not something that could be better changed in ourselves.

First take the beam out of your own eye, and then you will see
clearly to take out the speck that is in your brother's eye.

LUKE 6:42 AMP

I remember my mother's prayers and they have always followed me. They have clung to me all my life.

I prayed for this child, and the LORD has granted me what I asked of him.

1 SAMUEL 1:27 NIV

A problem not worth praying about isn't worth worrying about.

Be careful for nothing; but in every thing by prayer and supplication with thanksgiving let your requests be made known unto God.

PHILIPPIANS 4:6

Any child will learn to worship God
who lives his daily life with
adults who worship Him.

He who walks with the wise grows wise.

PROVERBS 13:20 NIV

Look around you and be distressed,
Look within you and be depressed,
Look to Jesus and be at rest.

Looking unto Jesus the author and finisher of our faith.

HEBREWS 12:2

A mother's love is patient and forgiving
when all others are forsaking,
and it never fails or falters,
even though the heart is breaking.

Love is patient, love is kind. It does not envy,
it does not boast, it is not proud. Love never fails.

1 CORINTHIANS 13:4,8 NIV

*M*aking children a part of a family team is of critical importance to the kinds of adults that they will become.

Behold, how good and how pleasant it is for brethren to dwell together in unity!

PSALM 133:1

*T*here is no greater love than the love that holds on where there seems nothing left to hold on to.

Love never fails [never fades out or becomes obsolete or comes to an end].

1 CORINTHIANS 13:8 AMP

*E*very mother is like Moses.
She does not enter the
promised land. She prepares
a world she will not see.

Then the LORD said to him, "This is the land I promised
on oath to Abraham, Isaac and Jacob. . . . I have let you see it
with your eyes, but you will not cross over into it."

DEUTERONOMY 34:4 NIV

God sends children for another purpose than merely to keep up the race—to enlarge our hearts, to make us unselfish, and full of kindly sympathies and affections.

My little children, let us not love in word, neither in tongue; but in deed and in truth.

1 JOHN 3:18

*E*very mother has the breathtaking privilege of sharing with God in the creation of new life. She helps bring into existence a soul that will endure for all eternity.

Thou didst form my inward parts;
Thou didst weave me in my mother's womb.

PSALM 139:13 NASB

We need to be patient with
our children in the same way
God is patient with us.

The discretion of a man deferreth his anger;
and it is his glory to pass over a transgression.

PROVERBS 19:11

A child is a gift whose worth cannot be measured except by the heart.

Behold, children are a gift of the LORD,

The fruit of the womb is a reward.

PSALM 127:3 NASB

My mother said to me, "If you become a soldier you'll be a general; if you become a monk you'll end up as the pope." Instead, I became a painter and wound up as Picasso.

(Love) . . . believeth all things, hopeth all things, endureth all things.

1 CORINTHIANS 13:7

*O*ur children are watching us live,
and what we are shouts louder
than anything we can say.

In everything set them an example by doing what is good.

TITUS 2:7 NIV

*H*appy is the child . . . who sees
mother and father rising early,
or going aside regularly,
to keep times with the Lord.

Let the heart of them rejoice that seek the LORD. *Seek the* LORD,
and his strength: seek his face evermore.

PSALM 105:3-4

You can do everything else right as a parent, but if you don't begin with loving God, you're going to fail.

The Lord our God is one Lord: and thou shalt love the Lord thy God with all thine heart, and with all thy soul, and with all thy might.

DEUTERONOMY 6:4-5

Beautiful as seemed mama's face,
it became incomparably more lovely
when she smiled, and seemed
to enliven everything about her.

The joy of the LORD is your strength.

NEHEMIAH 8:10

Daily prayers will diminish your cares.

Evening, and morning, and at noon, will I pray,
and cry aloud: and he shall hear my voice.

PSALM 55:17

*M*ercy among the virtues is
like the moon among the stars . . .
It is the light that hovers
above the judgement seat.

Mercy triumphs over judgment.

JAMES 2:13 NASB

*N*othing has a better effect upon children than praise.

Anxiety in the heart of a man weighs it down,
But a good word makes it glad.

PROVERBS 12:25 NASB

A house without love may be
a castle, or a palace, but it is
not a home; love is the
life of a true home.

Better a dry crust with peace and quiet
than a house full of feasting, with strife.

PROVERBS 17:1 NIV

*M*any a man has kept
straight because his
mother bent her knees.

*The earnest prayer of a righteous man
has great power and wonderful results.*

JAMES 5:16 TLB

The more a child becomes
aware of a mother's willingness
to listen, the more a
mother will begin to hear.

A wise man will hear, and will increase learning;
and a man of understanding shall attain unto wise counsels.

PROVERBS 1:5

I remember leaving the hospital . . . thinking, "Wait, are they going to let me just walk off with him? I don't know beans about babies!"

If any of you lack wisdom, let him ask of God, that giveth to all men liberally, and upbraideth not; and it shall be given him.

JAMES 1:5

A sweater is a garment
worn by a child when
his mother feels chilly.

She has no fear of winter for her household,
for she has made warm clothes for all of them.

PROVERBS 31:21 TLB

Fingerprinting children is a good idea.
It will settle the question
as to who used the guest towel
in the bathroom.

*Test everything that is said to be sure it
is true, and if it is, then accept it.*

1 THESSALONIANS 5:21 TLB

*A*ny mother could perform
the jobs of several air-traffic
controllers with ease.

She looketh well to the ways of her household,
and eateth not the bread of idleness.

PROVERBS 31:27

*P*arents must get across the
idea that, "I love you always,
but sometimes I do not
love your behavior."

Those whom I love, I reprove and discipline;
be zealous therefore, and repent.

REVELATION 3:19 NASB

*L*evel with your child by being honest. Nobody spots a phony quicker than a child.

In all things willing to live honestly.

HEBREWS 13:18

As parents, we never stand
so tall as when we stoop
to help our children.

Be humble, thinking of others as better than yourself.
Don't just think about your own affairs,
but be interested in others, too, and in what they are doing.
Your attitude should be the kind
that was shown us by Jesus Christ.

PHILIPPIANS 2:3-5 TLB

A good laugh is
sunshine in a house.

The light in the eyes [of him whose heart is joyful]

rejoices the hearts of others.

PROVERBS 15:30 AMP

Each loving act says loud and clear,
"I love you. God loves
you. I care. God cares."

Beloved, let us love one another: for love is of God;
and every one that loveth is born of God . . . for God is love.

1 JOHN 4:7-8

Children have more need of models than of critics.

Be their ideal; let them follow the way you teach and live; be a pattern for them in your love, your faith, and your clean thoughts.

1 TIMOTHY 4:12 TLB

It is better to keep children to their duty by a sense of honor and by kindness than by fear.

Do not irritate and provoke your children to anger [do not exasperate them to resentment], but rear them [tenderly] in the training and discipline and the counsel and admonition of the Lord.

EPHESIANS 6:4 AMP

(*E*ncouragement) is the art of "turning your children on," helping them to do for themselves, not doing for them.

And thou shalt teach them ordinances and laws, and shalt show them the way wherein they must walk, and the work that they must do.

EXODUS 18:20

*H*ome, sweet home—where each lives
for the other, and all live for God.

For none of us lives to himself alone and none of us dies to himself alone.
If we live, we live to the Lord; and if we die, we die to the Lord.
So, whether we live or die, we belong to the Lord.

ROMANS 14:7-8 NIV

Children have never been very good at listening to their elders, but they have never failed to imitate them.

As ye know what manner of men we were among you for your sake. And ye became followers of us.

1 THESSALONIANS 1:5-6

A baby is God's opinion that the world should go on.

God blessed them, and God said unto them, Be fruitful, and multiply, and replenish the earth, and subdue it.

GENESIS 1:28

A mother . . . fills a place so great that there isn't an angel in heaven who wouldn't be glad to give a bushel of diamonds to come down here and take her place.

The angel came in unto her, and said, Hail, thou that art highly favoured, the Lord is with thee: blessed art thou among women.

LUKE 1:28

I have held many things in my hands and lost them all; but the things I have placed in God's hands, those I always possess.

I know whom I have believed, and am persuaded that he is able to keep that which I have committed unto him against that day.

2 TIMOTHY 1:12

A mother is the one who is
still there when everyone
else has deserted you.

If you love someone you will be loyal to him no matter what the cost.

1 CORINTHIANS 13:7 TLB

A good deed is never lost;
he who sows courtesy reaps friendship,
and he who plants kindness gathers love.

*Whatsoever a man soweth, that shall he also reap. And let us not be
weary in well doing: for in due season we shall reap, if we faint not.*

GALATIANS 6:7,9

*E*very word and deed of a
parent is a fiber woven into
the character of a child that
ultimately determines how that child
fits into the fabric of society.

You will be judged on whether or not you are doing what
Christ wants you to. So watch what you do and what you think.

JAMES 2:12 TLB

*W*hen people ask me what I do,
I always say I am a mother first.

Many women do noble things, but you surpass them all.

PROVERBS 31:29 NIV

I think that saving a little child
And bringing him to his own,
Is a derned sight better business
Than loafing around the throne.

The fruit of the righteous is a tree of life;
and he that winneth souls is wise.

PROVERBS 11:30

A mother's patience is like
a tube of toothpaste—
it's never quite gone.

Being strengthened with all power according to his glorious might so
that you may have great endurance and patience.

COLOSSIANS 1:11 NIV

The school will teach children how
to read, but the environment of
the home must teach them what to read.
The school can teach them how to
think, but the home must teach
them what to believe.

Teach a child to choose the right path,
and when he is older he will remain upon it.

PROVERBS 22:6 TLB

Think of the sacrifice your mother had to make in order that you might live. Think of the sacrifice God had to make that you and your mother might live.

This is love: not that we loved God, but that he loved us
and sent his Son as an atoning sacrifice for our sins.

1 JOHN 4:10 NIV

*K*ind words can be short
and easy to speak, but their
echoes are truly endless.

She opens her mouth in skillful and godly Wisdom, and on her tongue
is the law of kindness [giving counsel and instruction].

PROVERBS 31:26 AMP

*G*od has given you your child,
that the sight of him, from time
to time, might remind you
of His goodness, and induce
you to praise Him with filial reverence.

See how very much our heavenly Father loves us, for he allows
us to be called his children—think of it—and we really are!

1 JOHN 3:1 TLB

*Y*our children learn more of your faith
during the bad times than they do
during the good times.

Consider it all joy, my brethren, when you encounter various trials.

JAMES 1:2 NASB

A woman who can cope with the "terrible twos" can cope with anything.

The Lord is on my side; I will not fear: what can man do unto me?

PSALM 118:6

*P*arenthood is a partnership
with God. . . . You are working
with the Creator of the universe
in shaping human character
and determining destiny.

We are labourers together with God.

1 CORINTHIANS 3:9

Who ran to me when I fell,
And would some pretty story tell,
Or kiss the place to make it well?
My mother.

As one whom his mother comforted, so will I comfort you.

ISAIAH 66:13

$\mathcal{R}$emember, when your child has a tantrum, don't have one of your own.

Every man that striveth for the mastery is temperate in all things.

1 CORINTHIANS 9:25

*T*he only thing children
wear out faster than shoes
are parents and teachers.

He gives power to the tired and worn out, and strength to the weak.

ISAIAH 40:29 TLB

A little boy, age eight, gave a profound definition of parenthood: "Parents are just baby-sitters for God."

I prayed for this child, and the LORD has granted me
what I asked of him. So now I give him to the LORD.
For his whole life he will be given over to the LORD.

1 SAMUEL 1:27-28 NIV

My mother was the source
from which I derived the
guiding principles of my life.

Be ye followers of me, even as I also am of Christ.

1 CORINTHIANS 11:1

*H*UMOROUS QUOTES SECTION

A merry heart doeth
good like a medicine.

PROVERBS 17:22

There is a right time for
everything: A time to laugh.

ECCLESIASTES 3:1,4 TLB

*N*ever lend your car to anyone
to whom you have given birth.

A merry heart doeth good like a medicine.

PROVERBS 17:22

*P*arenthood: that state of being better chaperoned than you were before marriage.

There is a right time for everything: A time to laugh.

ECCLESIASTES 3:1,4 TLB

The best way to keep children at home is to make home a pleasant atmosphere— and to let the air out of the tires.

A merry heart doeth good like a medicine.

PROVERBS 17:22

A mother finds out what is meant by spitting image when she tries to feed cereal to her baby.

There is a right time for everything: A time to laugh.

ECCLESIASTES 3:1,4 TLB

A lot of parents pack up their troubles and send them off to summer camp.

A merry heart doeth good like a medicine.

PROVERBS 17:22

*A*dult education is something
that will continue as long
as kids have homework.

There is a right time for everything: A time to laugh.

ECCLESIASTES 3:1,4 TLB

*S*mall boy: "If I'm noisy they give me a spanking . . . and if I'm quiet they take my temperature."

A merry heart doeth good like a medicine.

PROVERBS 17:22

Parents of teens and parents of babies have something in common. They spend a great deal of time trying to get their kids to talk.

There is a right time for everything: A time to laugh.

ECCLESIASTES 3:1,4 TLB

*P*eople who say they sleep like
a baby usually don't have one.

A merry heart doeth good like a medicine.

PROVERBS 17:22

A perfect example of minority rule
is a baby in the house.

There is a right time for everything: A time to laugh.

ECCLESIASTES 3:1,4 TLB

*I*f evolution really works,
how come mothers have
only two hands?

A merry heart doeth good like a medicine.

PROVERBS 17:22

The best time to give children your advice is when they are young enough to believe you know what you are talking about.

There is a right time for everything: A time to laugh.

ECCLESIASTES 3:1,4 TLB

*C*hildren are a great comfort
in your old age—and they
help you reach it faster, too.

A merry heart doeth good like a medicine.

PROVERBS 17:22

The quickest way for a parent
to get a child's attention is to
sit down and look comfortable.

There is a right time for everything: A time to laugh.

ECCLESIASTES 3:1,4 TLB

*M*an has his will—
but woman has her way.

A merry heart doeth good like a medicine.

PROVERBS 17:22

A food is not necessarily essential just because your child hates it.

There is a right time for everything: A time to laugh.

ECCLESIASTES 3:1,4 TLB

Cleaning your house while
your kids are still growing
is like shoveling the walk
before it stops snowing.

A merry heart doeth good like a medicine.

PROVERBS 17:22

A baby is an angel whose wings
decrease as his legs increase.

There is a right time for everything: A time to laugh.

ECCLESIASTES 3:1,4 TLB

A suburban mother's role is to
deliver children obstetrically once,
and by car forever after.

A merry heart doeth good like a medicine.

PROVERBS 17:22

*A*ny time a child can
be seen but not heard,
it's a shame to wake him.

There is a right time for everything: A time to laugh.

ECCLESIASTES 3:1,4 TLB

*I*nsomnia: a contagious
disease often transmitted
from babies to parents.

A merry heart doeth good like a medicine.

PROVERBS 17:22

ACKNOWLEDGEMENTS

Charles H. Spurgeon (7, 36), Ruth Bell Graham (8), Thomas Fessenden (10), Elbert Hubbard (11), V. Gilbert Beers (12), Hazel Scot (14), Dorothy Law Nolte (15), A. W. Thorold (16), Henry Ward Beecher (17, 65, 68), John A. Shedd (18), Whately (19), Penelope Leach (20), James Dobson (21, 31, 53), Wilfred A. Peterson (23, 29, 91), Mary Cholmondeley (24), Earl Riney (27), Dr. Anthony P. Witham (28, 72, 107), James Russell Lowell (30, 45), Mary Lamb (32), Mary Kay Blakely (33), Jean Hodges (35), Sydney J. Harris (37), George M. Adams (40), John J. Plomb (41), Jessamyn West (42), T. L. Cuyler (43), Abraham Lincoln (44, 78), Charles Meigs (49), Henry Wadsworth Longfellow (50), Dorothy Canfield Fisher (51), Lin Yutang (52), Henry Home (54), Franklin Roosevelt (55), Don Herold (56), Helen Pearson (60), Joseph Addison (62), Syrus (63), Lady Bird Johnson (64), Shannon Fife (66, 157), Mildred B. Vermont (69), Harold S. Hulbert (71), Peter Marshall (75), Barbara Bush (76), C. G. Jung (77), Anna B. Mow (80), Helen Steiner Rice (82), Dr. William Mitchell and Dr. Charles Paul Conn (83, 112), G. W. C. Thomas (84), Pope Paul VI (85), Mary Howitt (86), James Keller (87), Renee Jordan (88), Theresa Ann Hunt (89), Pablo Picasso (90), Larry Christenson (92), Alvin Vander Griend (93), Leo Tolstoy (94), Betty Mills (95), Edwin Hubbel Chapin (96), Sir P. Sidney (97), John Lubbock (98), Anne Tyler (101), Barbara Johnson (102), Lisa Alther (104), Amy Vanderbilt (105), M. MacCracken (106), Thackeray (108), Joyce Heinrich and Annette LaPlaca (109), Joseph Joubert (110), Terence (111), T. J. Bach (113), James Baldwin (114), Carl Sandburg (115), Billy Sunday (116), Earline Steelburg (117), St. Basil (119), David Wilkerson (120), Jacqueline Jackson (121), John Hay (122), Charles A. Wells (124), Mother Teresa (126), Christian Scriver (127), Beverly LaHaye (128), Judity Clabes (129), Ruth Vaughn (130), Ann Taylor (131), Dr. J. Kuriansky (132), John Wesley (135), Erma Bombeck (137), Madeline Cox (138), Dorothy Parker (139), Imogene Fey (140), Raymond Duncan (141), Coronet (143), Paul Swets (144), Leo J. Burke (145), Ed Dussault (147), Lionel M. Kaufman (149), Lane Olinhouse (150), Oliver Wendell Holmes (151), Katherine Whitehouse (152), Phyllis Diller (153), Peter DeVries (155).

Additional copies of this book and other titles
in the *God's Little Instruction Book* series
are available from your local bookstore.

God's Little Instruction Book, leather edition
God's Little Instruction Book for Men, leather edition
God's Little Instruction Book for Women, leather edition

If you have enjoyed this book, or if it has impacted your life,
we would like to hear from you. Please contact us at:

Honor Books
Department E
P. O. Box 55388
Tulsa, Oklahoma 74155

Or by e-mail at: info@honorbooks.com